250 BOATING QUESTIONS
Answered by Experts

250
BOATING QUESTIONS
Answered by Experts

Edited by
TOM BOTTOMLEY

Ziff-Davis Publishing Company
New York

Library of Congress Catalog Card Number 60-8223

Manufactured in the United States of America

To John West Bottomley, who started
my interest in boating by constructing
a working model of a full-rigged ship
and a steam-powered toy battleship,
both of which are still around after
thirty years of service.

PREFACE

Boatowners, even those who have been around the water for a long time, are always looking for information on how to get the best service from their craft. Non-owners' exposure to boat shows and advertising often leads them to decide to try the sport, but they are puzzled as to how to select the right craft and accessories for their needs from the bewildering array of possible choices.

The 250 questions included in this book are those most frequently asked by both newcomer and veteran (except for a few "ringers" I put in to clarify a point or to provide additional helpful information). The questions are arranged by subject: boat selection, engine selection, boat maintenance, engine maintenance, sails and rigging, seamanship, cruising techniques, and sources of free, money-saving information.

Answers are based on information that has appeared in articles and columns in *Popular Boating* Magazine. The experts include the *Popular Boating* staff—William T. McKeown, editor; Tom Bottomley, managing editor; and John L. Duffett and Philip Reavis, associate editors —and contributors to the magazine—Robert J. Shekter, Ellison Michel, Hank Wieand Bowman, John Kingdon, Nelson Borland, Bob Whittier, Elbert Robberson, R. J. Eckhart, H. A. Calahan, Capt. Jeremiah Whittaker, John R. Whiting, Jim Emmett, Nicholas Rosa, and Ann Davison—and the United States Coast Guard.

T.R.B.

CONTENTS

CONTENTS

250 BOATING QUESTIONS
Answered by Experts

CHAPTER

∾ 1 ∾

BOAT
SELECTION

EXPERTS

Nelson Borland
Tom Bottomley
Hank Wieand Bowman
John L. Duffett
John Kingdon
Ellison Michel
Robert J. Shekter

Selecting the right boat, particularly for a newcomer to the sport, can be a problem. The questions and answers here provide an outline of the boat types, construction methods, features to check in making a choice, and the methods of testing a boat. The advice is good for both new and used boats.

1

1 ⟿ In selecting an outboard boat, what should be considered first?

Select a boat made by a reputable builder. It is a good practice to choose a hull style that has been proved to be seaworthy on local waterways and that performs well under the conditions in which you expect to use it. Some factors to look for include self-bailing motor well, safety-glass or plastic windshield, and adequate built-in flotation on fiberglass or metal hulls. You must be certain that the transom is strong enough to take the desired outboard horsepower and that seating or cabin arrangements are adequate for your requirements.

2 ⟿ What should be considered first in buying an inboard boat?

Choose a boat built by a reputable manufacturer in a style that is suitable not only for local waters, but also for possible long trips. It is wise to select a hull made of material that stands up well under local conditions, and in a style that will be pleasing to you in the years to come. The boat should be powered to give you the speed and cruising range you desire. Check for adequate cockpit and cabin accommodations for cruising and family entertainment.

3 ⟿ In choosing a sailboat, what should be considered first?

Select a boat that is suitable for local waters. It should be similar to types you have already sailed so that you will feel comfortable about your ability to handle it. If you intend to sail it single-handed, be sure that the boat is not too big or too awkward to handle. Ease of maintenance and repair should be checked as well as allowance for making adjustments to rigging. If the boat is to be sailed by a family crew, sails and rigging should not be too complicated to handle. Sails should be made by a reputable sailmaker.

If the boat is to be raced, select a class that is popular in your area so that you will be assured of competition. Be sure that hull, sails, and rigging meet class specifications and that the sail inventory meets all racing requirements.

If the boat is to be used for cruising, cockpit and cabin accommodations should fit your family's needs. Provision should be made for heating the cabin in cool weather and ventilating it in warm weather. The boat should be equipped with auxiliary power, either inboard or outboard. Choose a hull design that will be safe and comfortable in a blow.

4 ∾ What do the terms "utility," "runabout," "cruiser," "express cruiser," and "flying-bridge cruiser" mean in reference to powerboat design?

Utility boats are usually small outboard-powered craft without any deck or cabin structure. Size range is generally 12 to 16 feet in length. Runabouts have decks forward and, occasionally, centerdecks or afterdecks. A cruiser is a boat equipped with a cabin. Motor and steering controls are located forward in the cabin. An express cruiser has the controls located outside the cabin at the after end, with a windshield on the cabin top. A flying-bridge cruiser is usually a fairly large craft, more than 30 feet in length, with one set of controls located in the bridge cabin and a second set of controls in a bridge mounted above the cabin. (See Figure 1–1.)

5 ∞ There has been a lot of talk about catamarans lately. What are some of the advantages and disadvantages in twin hulls for powerboats and sailboats?

Catamarans have rapidly gained popularity in the past two years. With power, they have proved to be fast and stable in rough going. Sailing cats are also extremely fast for their size, especially down wind. Since most power catamarans have room for twin-engine installations, construction must be rugged to take the resulting strains. Cockpit and cabin accommodations are somewhat limited in comparison to single-hull craft. Sailing catamarans have shown relatively poor performance in light airs, in tacking, and in going to windward. All of these negative characteristics are undergoing constant improvement, however, as naval architects and designers are turning their skills to the construction of this type of boat. (See Figure 1–2.)

6 ∽ What is a displacement-type hull?

A displacement-type hull is one that pushes aside, or displaces, a weight of water equal to the gross weight of the hull when the boat is in motion. Sailboats (except for a few planing types), ocean liners, tugboats, and barges are all examples of displacement-hull vessels.

7 ∽ What is a semiplaning hull?

A semiplaning hull lifts toward the surface of the water and becomes partially air-borne after the boat reaches a certain speed. The hull then displaces less than its total weight in the water. The bottom of the hull has a slight dead rise all the way back to the transom. You will find most powerboats, runabouts, and cruisers to be this type.

8 ∽ What is a true planing hull?

A true planing hull is one that tends to lift completely free of the water at high speed. The bottom of the boat, called the "planing surface," is completely flat—it has no dead rise—aft of the boat's center of gravity. "Cracker-box" racing hulls are of this type.

9 ∽ What is a hydroplane?

A hydroplane is a boat with more than one planing surface or "step." Most are now of the "three-point" type with two planing surfaces forward, called "sponsons," and one aft. Unlimited Class boats, such as the Gold Cup racers, are of this type. At high speed they often become completely air-borne except for the bottom half of the propeller!

10 ⚭ What determines the top speed a hydroplane is capable of attaining?

In a hydroplane, top speed is a matter of putting as much power as possible to work turning a correctly fitted propeller within the limits of class engine capacity requirements. Unlimited Class hydros, as the name implies, have no limit on the size of engine that can be used, and such craft have reached speeds in excess of 200 m.p.h. on straight runs. Sir Donald Campbell of England set a world's speed record on the water of more than 260 m.p.h. in his jet-engine-propelled *Bluebird*. At this writing, bandleader Guy Lombardo was tuning up his *Tempo Alcoa*, an aluminum-hulled hydroplane powered with an Allison J-35 jet engine, for an assault on this record in the spring of 1960.

11 ⚭ What determines the top speed of planing-type hulls?

A number of conditions are involved in determining speeds that semiplaning- and planing-type hulls can reach. These include the hull's displacement at top speed, its skin friction and wave-making resistance, and the efficiency of its engine and propeller.

12 ∽ What determines the top speed of a displacement-type hull?

The length of the hull at the waterline is the most important factor that governs the speed a displacement-type hull can make. A boat of given displacement with a long waterline will go faster than a shorter hull of the same displacement and, in some cases, will do it with less power. As a boat moves through the water, it sets up a wave system with one crest at the bow and a second crest somewhere aft along the waterline. As the boat speed increases, the distance between crests increases until it equals the waterline length of the hull. Slight increases in speed beyond this point would require fantastic increases in power.

The wave system set up by the boat is the manifestation of the pressure system created under the boat by the resistance it "meets" going through the water. As speed of the boat increases, this resistance increases gradually until, as noted above, the distance between wave crests equals the waterline length of the hull.

There is a definite relationship between speed and the

distance between crests of the wave system set up. These are "trochoidal" waves, the type that are formed when a pebble is dropped in a clear pool of water. After the pebble is dropped, a series of waves appears to move out from the point of impact. This motion is only apparent, as each particle of water merely moves up and down in one spot. But the speed of the apparent motion has been found to be exactly equal in knots (nautical miles per hour) to 1.34 times the square root of the distance (in feet) between adjacent crests. Distance between crests is determined by the diameter of the pebble dropped— or the waterline length of a boat at top speed. Height of the crests is determined by the weight of the dropped pebble—or the displacement of the boat.

The top speed of a boat with a waterline length of 45 feet would be about 9 knots (1.34 times the square root of 45 equals 8.978), and the top speed of a displacement hull with a waterline length of 55 feet would be about 10 knots.

13 ∞ What construction features should be checked on a carvel-planked hull?

Carvel, or plank-on-edge, construction is the most popular of traditional boatbuilding methods, especially for sailboats and larger cruisers. Check the size and materials used in such strength members as keel, keelson, stern, transom, and chines. Check the size of ribs and distance between centers, the thickness of hull planking, and the type of metal used for fastenings. The types of wood used in the hull and the kind of metal used in fastenings should be known to stand up well in local waters. Boats built of Scandinavian pine, for example, are more susceptible to rot and worm damage in the waters of the southern United States than boats planked with a good grade of mahogany. If a boat is to be used in salt water, bronze and Monel fastenings are required. Brass or cadmium-plated fastenings are suitable for use in freshwater craft.

14 ∽ What construction features should be checked in plywood-planked hulls?

Check the size and material used for strength members, the number of fore-and-aft stringers, the distance between frames, and the thickness and type of plywood used. Plywood should be marine or exterior grade and at least ⅜-inch thick on the bottom of any boat more than 14 feet in length.

15 ∽ What construction features should be checked in a lapstrake or "clinker-built" hull?

Check material used for the strakes. Northern white cedar is best, but because of its scarcity many boats are now planked with mahogany or plywood laps. In a plywood-planked boat, an elastic seam compound must be used between laps. The boat should be fastened with nonferrous rivets along laps.

16 ∾ What construction features should be checked in an aluminum hull?

The hull should be of heavy-gage alloy suitable for use in salt water. The boat should be free of sharp edges that might cut the operator or his passengers. Decking should be painted to protect against glare. Check the amount and the placement of flotation; Styrofoam or polyurethane foam placed under seats will keep a swamped aluminum hull afloat, but will not prevent a boat from capsizing. Ideally, flotation should be placed high under the decks and cockpit coaming.

17 ∾ What durability features should be checked in fiberglass hulls?

Check the thickness of material and look for signs of delamination. The best construction has a high glass-to-resin ratio. Check for stiffening members that keep the hull from flexing. Make sure that there are no ragged edges. The exterior finish should be smooth, with a molded-in color. Check the amount and the placement of flotation, as for an aluminum hull.

18 ᧞ What are the advantages and disadvantages of wood-constructed, carvel-planked hulls?

ADVANTAGES: This type of construction lends itself to traditional lines. Because wood floats, additional flotation material is not required. Construction is strong, if built right, and minor repairs are not difficult to make. DISADVANTAGES: Wood must be finished with paint or varnish to protect it against dry rot. Seasonal painting is generally required, although new paints help to minimize maintenance.

19 ᧞ What are the advantages and disadvantages of lapstrake construction?

ADVANTAGES: Lapstrake hulls are strong and leakproof, if properly built. Heavy ribs are not needed. This type is very popular for offshore powerboats. DISADVANTAGES: Seasonal painting is needed. If plywood laps are used, edges must be sealed to prevent possible delamination or rot.

20 ᧞ What are the advantages and disadvantages of plywood construction?

ADVANTAGES: Plywood boats are strong, durable, and relatively inexpensive. Built-in flotation is not required. DISADVANTAGES: Seasonal painting is required to protect against rot, and the material cannot be used where compound curves are designed into a hull.

21 ∽ What are the advantages and disadvantages of aluminum hull construction?

ADVANTAGES: Aluminum is lightweight, strong, and durable. The material can be formed to compound curves. DISADVANTAGES: Flotation units must be built into the hull, and the alloy must be resistant to corrosion. Repairs are difficult to make.

22 ∽ What are the advantages and disadvantages of fiberglass construction?

ADVANTAGES: One of the newest of boat construction materials, fiberglass lends itself well to compound curves. It is strong and lightweight, and color can be molded into the material. Damage to fiberglass is fairly easy to repair. DISADVANTAGES: Added flotation must be built in. Layup of material must be free of voids which tend to delaminate.

23 ∽ How can I test the performance of a powerboat?

First, find out if you are covered by the boat's insurance. If not, take out a 1-day policy for your own protection.

Be sure that all other legal equipment requirements are met. Pump the bilges. Check engine oil, fuel, and water. Turn on the ignition and check ammeter for deflection that would indicate a short circuit. Check engine operation, water flow, temperature, and gear shift operation. Check the boat's angle of trim under way. Check for engine vibration and boat stability at speed. Test for skidding or outward heel in slow turns—both can be dangerous. The boat should heel slightly to the inside of a turn. Check for pounding when crossing a wake at high speed. Check helm response at dead slow speed. Check accessibility of anchor and mooring lines. Check bilges again at the end of the test.

24 ∞ What do the terms "catboat," "sloop," "cutter," "ketch," "yawl," and "schooner" mean in reference to sailboat rigs?

A catboat has a single mast mounted well forward and carries no sail in front of the mast. Sailing dinghies are usually "cat" rigged. A sloop has a single mast, stepped fairly far forward, and carries one sail ahead of the mast in addition to the mainsail. A cutter has a single mast, usually stepped farther aft than on a sloop, and can carry two headsails on separate forestays. A ketch has two masts. The taller mast is forward, the smaller mast aft, but ahead of the rudder post. A yawl is similar to a ketch, but the aftermast is stepped behind the rudder post and is usually smaller than the second mast on a ketch. In both cases, the forward mast is called the "mainmast" and the aftermast is called the "mizzenmast." A schooner has two or more masts, with the tallest mast stepped aft. (See Figure 1–3.)

25 ∾ What is the difference between a gaff sail and a Bermuda or "marconi" sail?

A gaff sail has four sides. The upper edge of the sail is carried by a stiffening spar called a "gaff." The Bermuda sail is triangular and does not have a gaff.

26 ∾ What is a masthead rig?

A masthead rig is one in which the top of a foresail—working jib or genoa—reaches the top of the mast. (See Figure 1–4.)

27 ∾ What is the difference between a full-keel sailboat and a centerboard sailboat?

A full-keel boat has a permanent, fixed keel, usually weighted at the bottom. If the boat takes a knockdown in a blow, the weight of the keel helps to right it. A centerboard is a wood or metal plate that is lowered through a housing in the hull to give the boat lateral stability. On a centerboard boat, the crew must shift to the windward side to help maintain balance, particularly on a small boat, when working to windward. In a boat running downwind, the centerboard can be raised to reduce underwater drag. Also, the position of the centerboard can be adjusted so that the boat will steer a straight course with little pressure on the helm.

28 ∞ What is a "flush-deck" boat?

A flush-deck boat has no cabin structure above the deck, although it may have skylights on the deck. An excellent example is John Potter's sloop *Touché*.

29 ∞ How can I sea-test a sailboat?

Check the operation of an auxiliary engine under power as outlined for powerboats (see 23, above). On a centerboard boat, check clearance between board and centerboard housing. On a full keel boat, check keel bolts for signs of "weeping" (rust streaks around bolts) indicating that keel has worked loose. Check rigging for corrosion. Look for frayed spots in sheets and halyards. Check condition of sails and sail tracks. Under way, test balance of helm and the boat's ability to work to windward without sliding off to leeward. Check boat's ability to come about.

30 ⟳ What services do yacht brokers offer?

A broker can help match the needs of a buyer against available boats at a price within the buyer's budget. The broker generally knows the history and past performance of boats offered for sale. He can arrange to have a boat surveyed and to obtain insurance to cover the buyer's needs. A broker can also set up charters for a boat owner and, of course, help to sell a boat.

31 ⟳ What services do marine surveyors provide?

A surveyor checks the condition of a boat for a prospective buyer. He examines the boat for evidence of dry rot, damage to structural members, and condition of engine, engine bed, and fastenings. He provides the buyer with a list of a boat's shortcomings so that the buyer can get an estimate of the cost of needed repairs. The buyer pays the cost of having the boat hauled out of the water for the surveyor as well as the surveyor's fee and transportation costs.

32 ⟳ What does the term "fully found" mean?

It means that a boat is in completely seaworthy condition and that it is equipped with all gear and accessories required for normal use, including galley equipment and bed linen.

CHAPTER

∽ 2 ∽

ENGINE SELECTION

EXPERTS

Tom Bottomley
John L. Duffett
Bob Whittier

These pages cover the advantages and disadvantages of the three major types of power plants available for pleasure craft: outboard, inboard gasoline, and inboard diesel engines. The relationship of the engine and propeller to boat performance and power requirements for different hulls are also discussed.

17

33 ∾ What factors should be considered in choosing
    outboard power?

ADVANTAGES: Portability and low cost were once the
biggest advantages of outboard engines. This is still true
for the smaller engines. Outboards have a high power-to-
weight ratio; their two-cycle design allows them to wind
up to high speeds without internal damage. With an outboard, there is no problem of thrust-bearing wear or
shaft alignment.

DISADVANTAGES: Higher fuel consumption compared to
inboard engines of similar power and necessity to mix oil
with gasoline are the major drawbacks. Large horsepower
motors are now too heavy to take off a boat by hand and
must be left in place all season.

34 ∾ In what range is outboard power available?

Outboard engines range from as low as 1 h.p. in some
British models to 80 h.p. motors produced in this country. With a twin installation, it is possible to have outboard propulsion of 160 h.p., if the boat is large enough
and strong enough to take this much load on its transom.
Over-powering a boat can be dangerous.

35 ∾ How should outboard-engine power be matched
    to boat size and type?

Obviously, the size and type of the hull and the use for which the boat is intended must all be considered. Here are some general considerations: Do not use more power than that recommended by the boat's manufacturer. For fishing on small lakes or rivers in displacement-type hulls up to 16 feet, use 3 to 7 h.p. motors. For offshore fishing, 10 to 45 h.p. is adequate for semiplaning hulls in the 12- to 17-foot range. For pulling water skiers, use 10 h.p. and up, depending on the size of the boat and the number of skiers customarily pulled. For outboard cruisers, 35 h.p. and up can be used in single or dual installations, again depending on size of boat, hull design, and local water conditions.

36 ∽ What is the largest pleasure boat that will take an outboard installation?

A few cruisers have been built that are more than 30 feet in length. With new motors offering more and more power, manufacturers and designers are coming up with larger cruisers with all the accommodations and comforts once considered exclusive to inboard design. (See Figure 2–1.)

37 ∽ Is there any advantage to a twin-engine installation of relatively low power compared to a single engine of the same total power?

Yes, safety and maneuverability are two advantages of this type of installation. If one engine quits, there is still enough power in the other one to do the job. In tight maneuvering, such as at a crowded dock, one engine can be reversed while the other is in forward to turn the boat in its own length.

38 ᐁ How does the angle of the motor's lower unit relative to the keel affect boat performance?

If the motor is tilted too far out from the transom, the bow tends to rise high and the boat porpoises. (See Figure 2–2A.) If the motor is tilted too far in, the bow tends to dig in, thus reducing both speed and safety. (See Figure 2–2B.) With the correct tilt adjustment, the propeller shaft is parallel to the line of the keel. The boat rides level, moves up onto plane easily, and doesn't porpoise. (See Figure 2–2C.) On smaller boats, the number and placement of passengers may change the lower-unit angle needed for best performance.

39 ᐁ Where should remote controls be placed on a small runabout?

Forward-mounted controls are suitable for the larger, beamy hulls, especially those equipped with an electric-starting motor. Boats less than 15 feet long should have controls mounted farther aft, particularly if the hull is fairly narrow. Any boat in this size range with a manual-starting motor should have controls mounted aft for stability, ease of operation, and comfort.

40 ∽ Can outboard motors be used as auxiliary power on small sailboats?

Yes, this is often done. On craft with a transom-mounted tiller, the motor bracket is offset to one side. If the transom is unsuited for a bracket, it may be mounted on the side of the hull.

41 ∽ Is it possible to rig an outboard motor on a standard canoe?

Outboard motor mount brackets are available that attach to the canoe gunwale. Also, most canoe manufacturers now offer models with square transoms, made expressly to take outboard power. In either case, the motor need not exceed 3 h.p.

42 ∽ What happens when a following sea swamps a motor? What should be done?

The motor itself is seldom swamped by a following wave, and will continue to run in the rare cases where this does occur. New engines would have to be submerged completely for several seconds before they would fail. If a boat with a low transom is stopped suddenly after running at high speed, however, the following wave may slosh in through the transom cutout. When this happens, keep the passenger weight forward while the boat is bailed or pumped dry. If you move aft, your weight, plus the weight of the water in the hull, will bring the transom even lower, making it more vulnerable to following waves.

43 ～ What determines the power rating of an outboard motor?

Horsepower is measured by standards set up by the Society of Automotive Engineers under supervision of the Outboard Boating Club of America or the American Power Boat Association. Some manufacturers use the peak power developed for rating purposes; others use a more conservative reading for their rating.

44 ～ Why are outboard motors all two-cycle design?

A two-cycle engine is rather lightweight compared to a four-cycle engine of similar power. The crankcase does not need to be below the pistons in order to hold lubricating oil because oil is carried in the fuel mixture, which enters the crankcase before entering the cylinders.

45 ᕦᕤ How does atmospheric pressure affect engine operation?

The denser air becomes (the greater its barometric pressure), the more oxygen it contains per cubic foot. Fuel must combine with oxygen in order to burn. If more oxygen is present, more fuel can be fed to the engine in each piston's "charge," resulting in more power on each firing stroke. As barometric pressure decreases (in higher altitudes for example), fuel mixture should be "leaned out" to prevent fouling spark plugs. Power decreases with a leaner mixture.

46 ᕦᕤ What are the advantages of inboard power?

The fuel consumption of inboard engines is less than that of outboard engines of the same horsepower. Outboard engines are not available in sizes sufficient to power larger craft, those above about 30 feet in length.

47 ᕦᕤ What are the advantages of inboard gasoline engines as compared to diesel engines?

Gasoline engines are less expensive than diesel engines and, in smaller power ranges, more available. Also, parts and service for gasoline engines have been found to be more easily obtainable.

48 ᘒ What are the advantages of diesel engines?

Fuel for diesels is cheaper than that for gasoline engines, and fuel consumption is less in comparable power ranges. Because of their heavy construction, diesels require fewer overhauls over the years.

49 ᘒ What are the advantages of twin-inboard installations?

As in the case of outboards, safety and maneuverability are the advantages of twin-inboard installations.

50 ᘒ What causes the annoying "throb" that occurs when running at cruising speed with a dual-engine installation?

In this case, the engines are not turning at the same r.p.m. Install dual tachometers and adjust the speed of one engine until it matches that of the other. The "throb" will disappear.

51 ᘒ What determines the correct reduction gearing to use between engine and propeller?

Engine efficiency must be matched to propeller efficiency for maximum speed or minimum fuel consumption at cruising speed. Fast, light boats can use a direct drive because less power is needed to move the craft up onto plane. Heavier boats need reduction gearing in order to deliver more power to the propeller.

52 ✊ What is the relationship between power developed by the engine and power delivered to the propeller?

A propeller is most efficient in only one r.p.m. range, and the propeller shaft should turn with maximum torque in

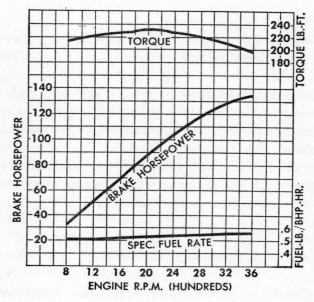

Figure A. ENGINE TORQUE CHART. (*Q. 52.*)

this range. This means that the engine should be geared to deliver its maximum torque at this propeller speed. This does not mean that the engine is reaching its peak horsepower. (See Figure A.)

53 ⤳ What determines the correct power for a displacement-type hull?

The power required is the minimum that will drive the boat at its maximum hull speed. More power would be wasted as any increase in speed would be negligible.

54 ⤳ What are the advantages of inboard engines with outboard drives?

These installations combine inboard economy with the flexibility of outboards. The engine is generally constructed so that the drive unit can be tilted or swung out of the way and the boat beached or trailered easily. One such unit mounts directly on the transom and requires no engine bed. It also features a tilting drive unit that swings up if an underwater obstruction is hit.

55 ⤳ What determines propeller size and pitch?

In general, propeller diameter and pitch are determined by the size and type of boat and the power delivered to the propeller shaft. Pitch determines the resistance to turning in the water that a propeller meets. For a specific answer to meet individual needs, see a reliable marine dealer.

56 ⌘ What are the advantages of water-jet propulsion for a boat?

Only one successful application of this type of propulsion for small craft has appeared on the market in this country. The Beuhler Turbocraft uses a three-stage axial-flow pump that draws water in through a grid on the bottom of the hull and forces it out through a "gate" on the transom. (See Figure 2–3.) Advantages include fast acceleration, extremely good maneuverability (steering is accomplished by a deflecting thrust of the water jet), and the ability of the boat to operate in extremely shallow water.

57 ⌘ What is the best way to have permanent gas tanks installed?

Fill pipe should be attached firmly to a tight deck plate. Fill pipe should extend to the bottom of the tank, with a well to form a liquid seal. Vent pipe should discharge to the open air outside the boat, away from all hull openings such as hatches, doors, windows, or ports. Outboard end of vent should be screened.

⚬ 3 ⚬

BOAT MAINTENANCE

EXPERTS

Tom Bottomley
H. A. Calahan
R. J. Eckart
Philip Reavis
Elbert Robberson

No boat is maintenance-free, in spite of new construction materials, and most owners take pride in the way they keep their craft in top condition. Questions and answers here cover the problems of spring fitting out and winter layup as well as general boat upkeep and repair. Engine maintenance is covered in Chapter 4.

58 ∽ What items in the hull interior should be checked at spring fitting-out time?

Examine cushions and other fabric-covered items for signs of mildew and treat where necessary with fungicide. Check for dry rot, especially under the ice chest and in poorly ventilated places. Clean bilges and limber holes and treat with oil or Cuprinol. Clean, prime, and paint woodwork as needed. Wash woodwork that is in good condition and paint, varnish, or wax as needed. Check condition of all through-hull fittings from the inside. Check through-deck fittings and all wiring. Inspect frames for splits or breaks in wood hulls.

59 ∽ What should be done to the hull exterior at spring fitting-out time?

On a wooden hull, remove old paint, sand wood, and caulk seams, if necessary. Remove paint and sand surface of a metal or fiberglass hull in poor condition. Check for dry rot or other damage to hull and repair as necessary. Check all hull fittings. Clean the bottom and prime wood or metal on topsides if necessary. Paint the hull with a good grade of marine paint. Examine the stern bearings to see if they need to be greased or adjusted. Examine the propeller and rudder assembly, making any necessary repairs. Apply antifouling paint to the bottom, and install anticorrosion electrodes just before launching. Touch up the waterline (boot-topping).

60 ∾ In fitting out for spring, what cabin equipment should be checked?

Inspect and repair upholstery and bedding. Overhaul galley stove, fresh-water pump, and marine toilet. Check the icebox for leaks. Check cabin lights and wiring. Be sure to have spare bulbs and fuses.

61 ∾ How should deck gear be checked at fitting-out time?

Overhaul deck winches. Adjust steering and engine controls. Check anchors and ground tackle, navigation lights and wiring, and mooring lines.

62 ∾ How should sailboat rigging be checked when fitting out?

Examine standing rigging for signs of corrosion and treat or replace as necessary. Turn halyards end for end, or replace if needed. Turn sheets end for end, or replace. Check all blocks and fairleads. Check masthead fittings. Check and lubricate turnbuckles. Adjust standing rigging to proper tension.

63 ∾ How should sails be checked?

Examine sails for rot and mildew, especially along the seams. Check the ties on batten pockets. Wash and "air out" sails and sail bags. Check the fit of battens and sand them smooth if necessary. Check mast slides. Make sure that you have enough sail stops and an emergency sewing kit.

64 ⚬ω What safety equipment should be checked at fitting-out time?

The medicine chest, including first-aid booklet or manual, should be checked, as well as all equipment required by the U. S. Coast Guard. Be sure to have distress signals, such as smoke signals and dye markers for daytime use and rockets and water lights for night emergencies. Get your Coast Guard Auxiliary Courtesy Examination.

65 ⚬ω In what sequence should painting be done on a boat?

Do interior painting first, then the exterior. Work from the top down. Thus, any spills won't mess up a freshly painted surface.

66 ⚬ω What is the correct way to prepare an "old" surface for painting?

Remove old paint with paint remover and/or a sander. A belt sander will take down paint on large surfaces. Vibrating or oscillating sanders can be used for fine work or for giving a "tooth" to paint that is still in good condition. (See Figure 3–1.) Fill digs, scrapes, and screw holes with putty; use 50-grit medium paper to sand smooth and feather edges. Use 120-grit, C-weight paper for clean-up sanding by hand on wood, fiberglass, or metal. Use a sanding block for all hand sanding.

67 ⌒⌢ What is the correct way to use paint?

Prepare the surface as outlined in 66, above. Do your painting on dry days, with the temperature between 40° and 80°. Check directions on the paint can and have paint well-shaken by your dealer no more than 48 hours before use. Pour enough paint for the job into a clean work can.

Use primer or sealer first on raw wood. On carvel-planked hulls, apply seam compound after the primer has dried. Sand the surface and clean with a tack rag (a rag dampened with turpentine). Apply a second coat of primer; sand and clean again when surface is dry.

Apply your first coat of paint. Do not thin paint, because this weakens it. If necessary, use a few drops of brushing liquid specified by manufacturer. Use a large brush and quick, smooth strokes. Watch for dribbling or gliding streaks. Sand and clean surface between coats.

68 ∞ How should bottom paint be applied?

Most bottom paints are applied directly over the bare wood. Buy the best bottom paint you can afford and read the directions on the can. Use a small brush with short, stiff bristles. (See Figure 3–2.) Do not add Paris Green or DDT to paint; this weakens its antifouling properties. Launch the boat while the paint is wet.

69 ∞ How should varnish be applied?

Do *not* shake the can. Slowly, to avoid bubbles, pour enough varnish for the job into a varnish cup. This cup should have a lip for draining your brush. Use as little brush action as possible and flow the varnish onto the surface. Do not reverse stroke back over a strip of varnish. Flow on strips of varnish adjacent to previous strips and work the edges together with a drained brush.

70 ∞ In preparing for winter storage, what items should be removed from a boat?

Instruments such as clocks and barometers and all electronic equipment such as radios and direction finders should be removed. All fabrics and any small wooden furnishings that can be refinished at home are also better taken from the boat. Remove all lines and all spars.

71 ↷ How should instruments and electronic equipment be treated and stored?

Dry out instruments under a lamp and wrap them in moisture-resistant paper. Store these items in a dry place.

72 ↷ What care should be given sails and other fabrics prior to storage?

Rinse all sails and fabrics in fresh water. Let them dry. Make any necessary repairs and mildew-proof cotton fabrics. Store fabrics in a dry place ashore.

73 ↷ What care should be given rope in the winter?

Wash rope and then dry and store it in a well-ventilated place ashore. (See Figure 3–3.)

74 ↷ How should spars such as the mast and the boom be stored?

Tag all spars with the name of your boat. Spars should be stored parallel to the ground and free from any sag between supports. (See Figure 3–4.) Remove any corrosion from rigging fittings and sail tracks. Lubricate the sail tracks.

Figure 1-1A. UTILITY. (Q. 4.)

Figure 1–1B. RUNABOUT. (Q. 4.)

Figure 1-1C. CRUISER. (Q. 4.)

Figure 1-1D. EXPRESS CRUISER. (*Q. 4.*)

Figure 1-1E. FLYING-BRIDGE CRUISER. (*Q. 4.*)

Figure 1-2A. POWER CATAMARAN. (*Q. 5.*)

Figure 1–2B. SAIL CATAMARAN. (Q. 5.)

Figure 1–3A. CATBOAT. (*Q. 24.*)

Figure 1–3B. SLOOP RIG. (*Q. 24.*)

Figure 1–3C. CUTTER RIG. (*Q. 24.*)

Figure 1–3D. KETCH RIG. (*Q. 24.*)

Figure 1–3E. YAWL RIG. (*Q. 24.*)

Figure 1–3F. SCHOONER. (*Q. 24.*)

Figure 1–4. MASTHEAD RIG. (Q. 26.)

Figure 2–1. OUTBOARD CRUISER. (*Q. 36.*)

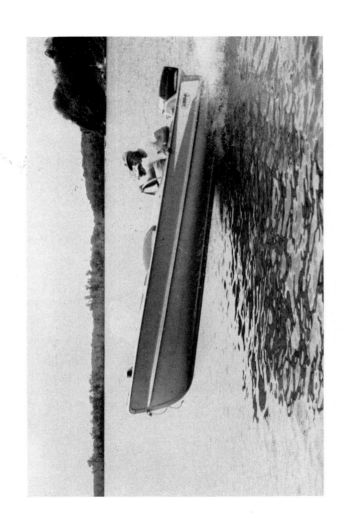

Figure 2–2A. HERE, THE MOTOR ANGLE IS TOO FAR AFT. (*Q. 38.*)

Figure 2–2B. HERE, THE MOTOR ANGLE IS TOO FAR FORWARD. (Q. 38.)

Figure 2–2C. HERE, THE MOTOR IS AT THE CORRECT ANGLE. (Q. 38.)

Figure 2–3. BUEHLER TURBOCRAFT. (*Q. 56.*)

Figure 3–1. A TIME-SAVING, VIBRATING SANDER. (*Q. 66.*)

Figure 3–2. BOTTOM PAINTING. (*Q. 68.*)

Figure 3–3. WASHED AND DRIED LINES, BEFORE STOWING. (*Q. 73.*)

Figure 3–4. CORRECT SPAR STORAGE. (*Q. 74.*)

Figure 3–5. WET STORAGE. (*Q. 75.*)

Figure 3–6. WINTER COVER. (*Q. 83.*)

Figure 3–7. CLEANING
THE BILGE. (*Q. 87.*)

Figure 4–1. OUTBOARD IGNITION CHECK. (*Q. 92.*)

Figure 4–2. OUTBOARD FUEL-SYSTEM SERVICE. (*Q. 93.*)

Figure 4–3. OUTBOARD LOWER-UNIT SERVICE. (*Q. 95.*)

Figure 4–4. AREA OF DIESEL AIR-INTAKE SERVICE. (*Q. 116.*)

Figure 6–1. HOISTING THE MAINSAIL. (*Q. 136.*)

Figure 6–2. POWERBOAT IN A TURN. (*Q. 143.*)

Figure 6–3. RUNNING AN INLET. (*Q. 146.*)

Figure 6–4. READING A COMPASS. (*Q. 164.*)

Figure 6–5. USING A SEXTANT
TO TAKE A RELATIVE BEARING.
(*Q. 166.*)

Figure 7–1. SAFETY-CONSCIOUS YOUNGSTERS OUT FOR A SPIN.
(*Q. 200.*)

Figure 7–2.   A GRILL MAKES FOR HOT MEALS WHEN CAMPING OUT.
(*Q. 219.*)

75 ∽ What are the advantages of "wet" storage?

In wet storage, the boat remains in the water all winter. The hull does not dry out or lose shape due to possible improper support. Wet storage is less expensive than storage ashore. (See Figure 3–5.)

76 ∽ How should a boat be prepared for wet storage?

Drain and plug all through-hull plumbing to protect against ice damage. Protect the hull's waterline against ice damage with wood or tire fenders. Rig chafing gear on mooring lines. Add plenty of rock salt to the bilge to prevent dry rot. Provide adequate ventilation under a protective cover.

77 ∽ What are the advantages of dry storage?

Accessibility of boat for inspection and work and its protection against ice and storms are the major advantages of storage ashore.

78 ∽ Is it proper to store small boats upside down to eliminate the need for a boat cover?

No. Even the smallest boats tend to work out of shape if stored upside down for the winter.

79 ∾ How should the average outboard runabout or cruiser be supported for winter storage?

The weight of the boat should rest on the keel. The keel should be supported by timbers that distribute the weight over a large area. Poppets—vertical timbers—balance the boat upright. Shims and wedges under poppets allow for adjustment as the ground "works" with alternate freezing and thawing. A properly adjusted trailer makes an excellent support for an outboard boat.

80 ∾ How should a centerboard sailboat be supported in dry storage?

Support it as for an outboard boat (see 79, above) and remove the centerboard.

81 ∾ How should supports be arranged under the hull of an inboard?

The weight of the hull should rest on its keel, as it does for outboards, with poppets used to balance the boat. Additional timbers should support the hull under the engine or engines to prevent the hull from sagging.

82 ∾ How should timbers be placed under the hull of a full-keel sailboat?

Again, the weight of the boat should rest on its keel, which is supported by timbers that distribute the weight over a wide area. Poppets are used to balance the boat. Additional poppets under the bow and stern overhangs are used to prevent the hull from "hogging" (sagging down at each end).

83 ⌇ How should a winter cover be set up for the best boat protection?

A cover should be set up in an inverted "V," with enough slant to prevent sagging due to accumulated snow or water. It should be lashed down tightly to prevent its blowing loose in high winds, and adequate ventilation should be provided under it. (See Figure 3–6.)

84 ⌇ How should ventilation be provided under a winter cover?

An open, overhanging eave can be placed at each end of the cover, or stove pipes can be installed at each end, with the ends of the pipes pointing down to keep out rain.

85 ⌇ What maintenance should be performed on the hull when a boat is hauled from the water for storage?

Scrub barnacles and other marine growth off the bottom with a stiff brush. Fill bare spots and gouges with trowel cement and apply a coat of paint over them to prevent dry rot.

86 ∽ What exterior fittings should be checked when the boat is hauled out of the water?

Inspect for bent or nicked propeller, loose struts, and worn shaft bearings. Plan for needed repairs and order any needed parts. Check propeller-shaft alignment and rudder fittings. Inspect all through-hull fittings and plumbing and examine all exterior fittings for corrosion.

87 ∽ What can be done to the interior of a hull at haul-out time to protect it and to reduce work that must be done in the spring?

Scrub and scrape the bilge and apply wood preservative. Inspect woodwork for rot. Repair and paint as needed. (See Figure 3–7.)

88 ∽ What care should be given deck hardware before storage?

Give hardware a good coat of grease. Coat it all in aluminum foil to prevent corrosion.

89 ෨ Is there any advantage to doing paint work in the fall?

Yes. If the hull finish is in good shape, touch-up painting can be done at this time. If it is in poor shape, touch up enough to protect the wood during the winter. A coat or two of varnish reduces springtime brightwork refinishing.

90 ෨ Are there any general tips on work to accomplish in the fall that will help save time in spring fitting out?

Order all necessary equipment at this time to avoid the delays that are likely to be encountered in the spring rush. Have engine work, plumbing, and electrical systems overhauled during the winter. Refinishing of small parts can be done at home.

ENGINE
MAINTENANCE

EXPERTS

Tom Bottomley
Hank Wieand Bowman
John L. Duffett
Philip Reavis

Here are questions and answers that deal with operation and maintenance of outboard, inboard gasoline, and inboard diesel engines. Seasonal work on electrical, fuel, water, and exhaust systems at spring fitting out and winter layup times is also covered, as well as care to be given propellers and drive shafts.

91 ⁀ Outboard engines are two-cycle motors. What are the principles of two-cycle gasoline-engine operation?

In a two-cycle gasoline engine, a fuel-air mixture from the carburetor enters the crankcase, where oil mixed with the fuel lubricates the crankshaft, piston-rod bearings, and cylinder walls. As the piston moves down on its firing stroke, this fuel charge is compressed slightly in the crankcase. As the piston nears the bottom of its stroke, an exhaust port opens, allowing burned gases to escape. At the bottom of the stroke, an intake port opens up and the crankcase fuel charge enters the cylinder. The charge is compressed as the piston moves up, and a fresh charge is drawn into the crankcase from the carburetor. The charge in the cylinder is fired as the piston reaches the top of its stroke, forcing the piston down. A flywheel provides the necessary momentum to cause the piston upstroke.

92 ⁀ What care should be given an outboard engine's ignition system?

Plugs should be kept clean and properly gapped. (See Figure 4–1.) Inspect high-tension leads from the magneto to the spark plugs for dirt and worn or frayed insulation. Electric-starter and generator wiring should be checked for dirt and fraying. Magneto work should be done by a competent serviceman.

93 ~ What service should the outboard motor's fuel
    system receive?

Check fuel lines and fittings for corrosion or leaks. Remove and clean the fuel filter at regular intervals (see
Figure 4–2) at least twice a season during normal operation. Use regular-grade gasoline with proper oil mixture
as specified in the engine manual to avoid fouling spark
plugs.

94 ~ What care should be given an outboard's cooling
    system?

Each time the motor is operated, check to make sure that
water is being circulated. If water is not coming out of its
outlet or "telltale" (an outlet that discharges part of the
cooling water to show that the water pump is function-
ing), stop the engine and have it checked by a serviceman. The fuel pump may be clogged or damaged. Flush
the cooling system in fresh water at least three times a
year, if the boat is operated the year around. Older-model
engines may need flushing after every use in salt water.

95 ~ What care should be given the engine's lower
    unit?

Lubricate according to the specifications found in the
owner's manual. In most cases, the lubricant is pumped

into a fitting low on the unit until it starts to run out an upper vent. (See Figure 4–3.)

96 ⤳ What care does the propeller require?

Inspect the propeller frequently for dents, nicks, or bent blades. Use a file to dress minor nicks. Bad dents or bent or broken blades mean that the propeller must be replaced.

97 ⤳ What care do remote controls require?

Lubricate linkage with SAE 30 oil and check for kinks and sharp bends in cables. Apply gear lubricant to gears and teeth of the control-unit mechanism at least once a year.

98 ⤳ What maintenance should be performed on the outboard motor prior to winter storage?

Remove the motor from the boat and flush the cooling system in fresh water. Drain the oil from the lower unit and flush with kerosene. Refill with correct lubricant. Drain fuel at the carburetor. Remove spark plugs and ground the leads to prevent damage to the magneto. Spray SAE 30 oil into cylinder heads, then replace spark plugs and spark-plug leads. Clean the outside of the motor with solvent. Clamp the motor upright in a dry place and wrap it in canvas or heavy paper.

99 ⟋ What are the principles of four-cycle inboard gasoline-engine operation?

(1) A fuel/air charge enters the cylinder on the down-stroke of the piston. (2) This charge is compressed on the upstroke. (3) The spark plug fires the charge, forcing the piston down. (4) Exhaust gases are forced out on the next upstroke. A heavy flywheel keeps the piston moving on all cycles except firing stroke and tends to dampen vibration on multiple-cylinder units (that is, on most marine engines), where at least one cylinder is firing during each half revolution of the crankshaft.

100 ⟋ What care should be given the ignition system on an inboard gasoline engine?

Inspect, clean, and gap the spark plugs as required by specifications in the owner's manual. Check high-tension wiring for dirt and abrasions. Check distributor points as well as rotor and distributor-cap contacts for pitting and corrosion. Check battery terminals, wiring to generator, and distributor. Inspect starter and generator brushes.

101 ⟋ What care should be given the fuel system?

Keep the fuel system clean. Check filter strainers in the fuel tank and at the engine. Check lines and fittings for worn spots or cracks that could start to leak. Clean the backfire trap at regular intervals.

102 ∾ How does a salt-water cooling system work?

A water pump circulates raw sea water through the engine's cooling passages, into the cylinder head and block, and back out to the sea.

103 ∾ What are the advantages and disadvantages of salt-water cooling?

The installation is less expensive than that of a heat-exchanger cooling system and is simple. However, engine cooling tends to be uneven because cold sea water heats up gradually as it passes from one end of the engine to the other; the temperature difference may be as much as 25°. Water-inlet passages must be kept small to restrict the flow of water so that the engine will not run too cool. Engine efficiency is best when operating in the 140° to 180° range, but with salt-water cooling, the operating temperature must be kept below 140° to prevent a build-up of salt deposits in the cooling system.

104 ∾ What care should be given a salt-water cooling system?

Check for leaks in the cooling system. Check the operating temperature each time the engine is used for evidence of overheating (above 140°).

105 ⚬↝ How does a fresh-water cooling system operate?

Fresh water is circulated through a closed circuit, as in an automobile, but a heat-exchanger unit replaces the automotive radiator. Sea water circulating through the heat exchanger cools the fresh water as it passes through this unit.

106 ⚬↝ What are the advantages and disadvantages of a heat-exchanger cooling system?

ADVANTAGES: A heat-exchanger system gives controlled, even cooling, which allows higher, more-efficient engine operating temperatures.
DISADVANTAGES: The installation is more complex and expensive than a salt-water cooling system.

107 ⚬↝ What care should be given a fresh-water heat-exchanger cooling system?

Check the system periodically for leaks. The heat exchanger can be removed for flushing when the boat is hauled.

108 ∞ What care should be given the inboard engine's exhaust system?

Check manifold bolts for tightness and inspect manifold gaskets for breaks or worn spots. Check manifold and exhaust pipes for leaks. Check water jackets for leaks on engines so equipped.

109 ∞ What maintenance should be given the propeller-shaft stuffing box?

Inspect the stuffing box for leaks. If the lag screws used for mounting the box work loose, bad leaks can result. Replace with larger lags if necessary, or plug the old holes and bore new ones for the lag screws.

110 ∞ How can the propeller be checked on an inboard rig?

It is best to check an inboard boat's propeller when the craft is hauled out of the water. By wearing a skin diver's face mask, however, it *is* possible to inspect the propeller while the boat is in the water. Check for dents, nicks, and bent or broken blades.

111 ∞ What should be done to a gasoline inboard engine in preparation for winter storage?

Drain the cooling system and flush it with fresh water. If a heat-exchanger system is used, refill it with water and antifreeze solution. Drain the water jackets on exhaust manifolds. Drain the crankcase, flush it thoroughly, and refill with winter lubricant. Remove spark plugs, pour about one cup of engine oil into each cylinder, and replace spark plugs. Remove and clean the fuel pump and carburetor; then replace. Remove and inspect the electrical equipment and store it in a dry place. Remove the battery and put it on a charger in the boat-yard shop or garage. Turn the engine over by hand several times during the winter to alter the tension on valve springs and lifters.

112 ∾ What should be done to the inboard gasoline engine at spring fitting-out time?

Check ignition, fuel, cooling, and exhaust systems as outlined in 111, above. Replace all electrical equipment and the battery. Drain engine crankcase of winter oil and refill with the correct grade of operating oil.

113 ∾ What are the principles of diesel operation?

Diesel engines may be two-cycle or four-cycle. Two-cycle operation is similar to the outboard gasoline engine, except that fuel is injected into the cylinder by a nozzle on the compression stroke (see 91, above). Four-cycle operation is similar to the four-cycle gasoline engine, except that fuel is injected into the cylinder by a nozzle and air enters separately through an intake valve. In both two- and four-cycle engines, the fuel charge is not ignited by a spark plug but by the heat generated in the compression stroke. To accomplish this, the compression ratios of diesel engines must be much higher than those for gasoline engines.

114 ∽ What care should be given the diesel fuel system?

Drain the fuel-injection pump governor housing periodically and refill to the proper level with a recommended type and grade of lubricating oil. Inspect and replace the fuel-filter elements as needed. Inspect and clean fuel strainers and filter housings. Check fuel lines and fittings for loose joints, worn spots, or cracks.

115 ∽ What care should be given the diesel cooling system?

Check the cooling system in a manner similar to that outlined for gasoline inboard engines (see 91, above).

116 ∽ What maintenance does the air-intake system require on a diesel engine?

Drain, clean, and refill the oil-bath air filters periodically. (See Figure 4–4.) Clean air-box drains, crankcase vent tube, and blower screen.

117 ∞ What care should be given the diesel exhaust system?

Follow the procedures outlined for gasoline inboard engine exhaust systems (see 110, above).

118 ∞ What maintenance should be performed on a diesel engine in preparation for winter storage?

Drain and flush the crankcase and refill it with the proper winter oil. Drain the fuel-injection pumps and governor housing and refill them with preservative oil. Drain the cooling system and close the drains and intake valves. Refill the system with an antifreeze solution. Seal off the air cleaner, exhaust pipes, and crankcase vent openings with tape or some other waterproof material.

119 ∞ What are the spring fitting-out procedures for a diesel engine?

Remove seals from air cleaners, exhaust pipes, and crankcase vent openings. Drain the antifreeze solution from the cooling system and refill it with fresh water. Drain preservative oil from crankcase, fuel-injection pumps, and governor housing. Refill with the proper type and grade of lubricating oils.

CHAPTER

ᗡᕀ5ᕀᗡ

RIGGING
AND SAILS

EXPERTS

Tom Bottomley
Elbert Robberson
Robert J. Shekter

Traditional materials (manila for rope, cotton duck for sails) still have their advantages and in some cases may outperform the new synthetics—Nylon and Dacron—which are used for both lines and sails. Here we cover the advantages and disadvantages of these rigging and sail materials and deal with rigging problems.

120 ∿ How much leverage, or mechanical advantage, does a block and tackle give?

Any advantage depends on the number of single blocks, or sheaves in pairs of blocks, and the resultant spans of

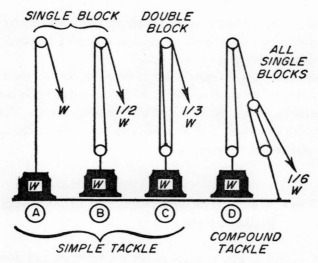

Mechanical force required to lift a given weight is illustrated. Compound tackle rig **D** needs only one sixth the pull needed at rig A.

Figure B. FORCES INVOLVED IN SIMPLE AND COMPOUND TACKLES. (*Q. 120.*)

line between the load-end block and the fixed block (see Figure B). Two single blocks reduce the pull needed to lift a given load by half. With a double block at the top, a single block at the load, and three spans of line between,

the pull needed to lift the load is one third that required
without a block-and-tackle rig.

121 ∽ What are the advantages and disadvantages of
       manila line?

ADVANTAGES: Manila line is relatively inexpensive, strong,
and does not stretch when used as sheets or halyards. It
is also relatively easy to splice.
DISADVANTAGES: Manila is not resistant to rot and mildew,
and it must be washed and dried before stowing. It is not
as strong as synthetic line of the same diameter. Manila
shrinks when wet and, if used as sheets or halyards, must
be slacked off in rain.

122 ∽ What are the advantages and disadvantages of
       synthetic lines?

ADVANTAGES: The synthetics are rot-resistant and do not
need to be dried before stowing. Nylon line is slightly
elastic and, thus, can be used for mooring and anchor
lines. Dacron lines do not stretch and can be used in any
application. Polyethylene lines float and are excellent
tow ropes for water skiers.
DISADVANTAGES: The initial cost of synthetic line is high
compared to manila, and elasticity of Nylon makes it
unsuitable for use as halyards. The slick fibers of syn-

thetic lines make them more difficult to splice than manila.

123 ✤ What are the names given the various lines on the average sailboat? What are their uses?

Halyards (or halliards) are used for hoisting objects, such as sails or pennants. *Sheets* control the angle of sails and take the name of the sail to which they are attached, such as main sheet and jib sheet (see Figure C). *Stays* support a mast from the bow and stern of a boat (forestays and backstays). *Shrouds* support a mast from the sides of a boat. *Lanyards* are lashed to an object such as a knife or whistle so that it can be carried on the person. *Mooring lines* are used to tie a craft to a pier. The line or chain fastened to an anchor is called the *anchor rode*. Rigging used to work a boat, such as halyards and sheets, is *running rigging*. Stays, shrouds, and other permanent rigging are all *standing rigging*.

124 ✤ What can be done to prevent an anchor line from chafing where it passes through the bow chocks?

The simplest way to prevent chafing is to wrap a piece of heavy cloth around the anchor line where it passes through the chocks, after lashing the cloth to the line with

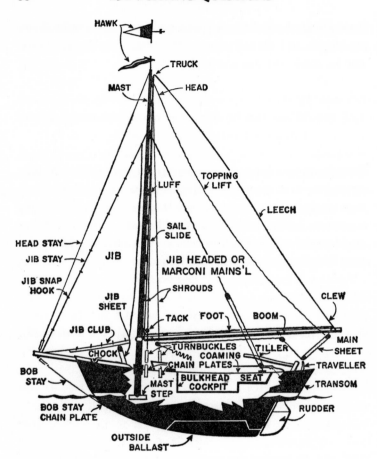

Figure C. SAILS AND RIGGING. (Q. 123.)

a winding of marline. A piece of hose can be split down its length and placed around the line, or a leather collar can be made for this purpose.

125 ∾ What can be done to extend the useful life of a line used for an anchor rode?

Because most anchor lines are fairly long—50 to 100 feet, or more—and most anchoring is done in relatively shallow water, only one end of the line gets much use during a season. At the end of the first season, "swap" the line end for end to get an extra season's use from it. Also, protect it against chafe, as in 124, above.

126 ∾ Why are sails made of several pieces of cloth sewn together instead of a single piece of cloth?

Fabrics are not made in widths suitable for cutting entire sails. Then too, seams serve to control the shape of the sail and give added strength at points of strain.

127 ∾ What are the proper names of the various edges and corners of a sail?

The forward edge of a sail is the *luff*, the after edge is the *leech*, and the bottom edge is the *foot*. The upper corner is called the *head*, the lower-forward corner is called the *tack*, and the lower-after corner is called the *clew*. (See Figure C.)

128 ൟ What are the advantages and disadvantages of cotton sails?

ADVANTAGES: Cotton sails are less expensive than those made of synthetic fabrics. In some one-design boat classes, they are required for racing by class specifications.

DISADVANTAGES: Cotton sails are neither mildew- nor rot-proof and must be dried thoroughly before stowing. Cotton sails also tend to wear out more quickly than synthetics.

129 ൟ What are the advantages and disadvantages of synthetic sails?

ADVANTAGES: Synthetic sails are lightweight, rot- and mildew-proof, and strong. They can be stowed while wet.

DISADVANTAGES: The initial cost of sails made from synthetic materials is higher than that of cotton sails. Nylon tends to stretch and is unsuited for use in sails other than spinnakers.

130 ൟ How long should sail battens be in relation to the sail batten pockets?

Battens should be about 1 inch shorter than the pockets; they should be tied securely in the pockets. A loose batten working its way out of a pocket in a blow can rip the sail.

131 ∾ What are sail stops?

Sail stops are heavy cotton straps used to lash the sail to the boom when the sail is furled.

132 ∾ What is the difference between Dacron sails and Terelyne sails?

The only difference is in the place where the sail material was made. Terelyne is the British name for Dacron.

133 ∾ What is the proper way to reef a sail, using reef points?

First, lash down the reef cringle at the tack of the sail and then lash down the reef cringle at the clew. Tie the reef points, starting at the mast and working aft. Reef points are tied between the foot of sail and the boom, not around the boom.

134 ∾ Are there any maintenance measures that can be taken to protect sails against wear?

If a boat is to be used on a long cruise where sails may remain set over long periods of time on the same tack, baggy wrinkle can be placed on rigging where sails chafe (see Figure D). Wooden or nylon roller guards can be placed around shrouds where genoas might chafe.

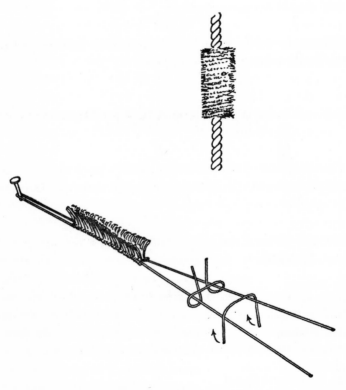

Figure D. BAGGY WRINKLE. (*Q. 134.*)

CHAPTER

❧ 6 ❧

SEAMANSHIP

EXPERTS

Jim Emmett
Ellison Michel
Elbert Robberson
John Whiting
Capt. Jeremiah Whittaker
The U. S. Coast Guard

Seamanship is the art of handling a boat in all conditions of wind and weather. It includes maneuvering a boat around a pier as well as anchoring techniques, piloting, and helmsmanship on open waters. The questions and answers that follow comprise our longest chapter because this subject is so important.

93

135 ∾ What is the proper way to leave a boat slip under power?

This depends on the location of the slip and the position of the boat in the slip. If the way ahead is clear, cast off the mooring lines and slowly proceed ahead and away from the dock. If the boat must be backed out, remember that a single-screw engine will tend to swing the stern to port; in any case, once clear of the pier, bring in the boat fenders.

136 ∾ What is the correct way to leave a mooring under sail?

Hoist the mainsail first (see Figure 6–1), then the jib. Leave both sheets slack and cast off the mooring. As the boat gathers speed sternway, back the tiller so that the boat will swing around with the wind on the side decided upon for the first tack. Haul in the jib sheet until the sail is drawing properly and then haul in on the mainsheet to set the mainsail.

137 ∾ What is the correct way to approach a dock or mooring under power?

Approach the mooring against the wind or current, whichever is stronger.

138 ᴑᴡ What is the correct way to pick up a mooring
when under sail?

Approach the mooring from down wind on a course
which would put the mooring about a boat's length to
windward if you were to continue on past it. On the approach, lower and secure the jib. When you reach the
point where the mooring is one boatlength to windward,
luff up into the wind. The boat's momentum allows it to
coast up to the pick-up buoy. Secure the mooring line
and lower and secure the mainsail.

139 ᴑᴡ How much anchor line should be let out when
you drop anchor?

Standard practice for normal anchoring is to allow 7 feet
of anchor line for every foot of water depth at low tide.
The length of line used is called the "scope." If weather
conditions are bad, or if the hook does not seem to be
holding, allow more scope.

140 ᴑᴡ Some anchors are fitted with a length of chain
to which the anchor rode is connected. What is
the purpose of this chain?

A length of chain helps an anchor dig in because it holds
the shank of the anchor down and parallel to the bottom.

Then too, if the anchored boat is surging up and down on heavy swells, the chain dampens the tugging action on the anchor line so that the hook remains set.

141 ⬿ What is the correct way to drop anchor when under power?

Select a desirable spot. Approach against the wind or current, whichever is stronger. The position of other boats at anchor will indicate this. Go about three boat-lengths past the selected spot (or enough beyond to give you a seven-to-one anchor-scope ratio when you drop back on the hook). Stop the boat's headway and lower the anchor until it reaches bottom. Back the boat slowly, paying out anchor line. As the boat moves back, shift into neutral and snub the anchor line around the mooring bitt or cleat. When the anchor takes hold, uncleat the anchor line and let the boat drop back to the desired spot as you pay out additional anchor line. When your spot has been reached, secure the anchor line and shut off the engine.

142 ⬿ What is the correct way to drop anchor when under sail?

Approach the spot where you want the boat to lie from down wind. When the spot is reached, luff up into the wind so that the boat will come to a stop about two or three boatlengths to windward of the spot. When forward movement has stopped, lower the anchor until it reaches bottom. As the boat starts to drop back, pay out on the anchor line. Snub the line around a cleat or the mooring bitts to set the anchor and then let the boat fall back to the selected spot. Secure the anchor line and lower and secure the jib and mainsail.

143 ∾ What is the action of a powerboat in a turn?

Unlike an automobile, where the rear wheels follow the path of the front of the car, a boat tends to pivot about a point forward of amidships. The stern, then, swings toward the outside of the turn. A boat should bank toward the inside of the turn. (See Figure 6–2.) A bank toward the outside of the turn is a dangerous design.

144 ∾ What is the best way to head an outboard cruiser into waves 4 to 6 feet high?

Head into the waves at a slight angle to avoid unpleasant and dangerous pounding. Maintain enough power to keep this heading because the action of waves tends to swing the boat broadside to them.

145 ∾ What is the best way to handle a semiplaning, hull-type boat in a blow?

Head into the waves, as described in 144, above, if possible. Do not try to maintain planing speed—the boat may not stand up under extremely heavy pounding. However, you should have sufficient power to keep the boat from turning parallel to the wave troughs.

146 ⟿ What is the best way to enter an inlet when a heavy following sea is running?

Remember that the action of waves may turn a boat broadside to them, which could lead to broaching (rolling over in a trough). Maintain enough speed to give good steering control, but do not go so fast that the boat runs down one wave and digs into the wave ahead. This could cause a boat to be "pitchpoled" end over end. (See Figure 6–3.)

147 ⟿ What is the color and number code of buoys that mark channels?

Nun buoys, spars, day markers, bells, whistles, and other aids to navigation that mark the starboard side of a channel when entering from seaward are red. Can buoys, spars, day markers, bells, whistles, and other aids to navigation that mark the port side of a channel when entering from seaward are black. Red markers are even-numbered and black markers are odd-numbered. Numbers run in sequence from seaward (black marker #1 and/or red marker #2) to land.

Black-and-white aids to navigation mark the middle of a channel; red-and-black aids mark the junctions of channels or underwater obstructions. These markers are not numbered.

148 ⚭ There are some channel markers on the East Coast that are normal except for yellow borders or bands on both red and black buoys. What are these?

These markers are aids to navigation on the IntraCoastal Waterway.

149 ⚭ What is the color code of channel lights?

Red, even-numbered aids to navigation show red lights. Black aids show white or green lights. In either case, the lights may be flashing or occulting. U. S. Coast & Geodetic Survey charts show light characteristics. Lights on junction markers may be red, white, or green. In any case, they are always quick, flashing lights. Midchannel markers show white lights that give short–long flashes.

150 ⚭ What is the difference between flashing and occulting lights?

Flashing lights blink on at intervals; occulting lights blink off at intervals.

151 ᧤ What are ranges?

Ranges are two or more markers on shore—sometimes prominent landmarks—that give a line of position.

152 ᧤ What information is carried on charts?

All that the boat operator needs to know for accurate and safe piloting in the area covered is shown on a chart, except for tide information and radio-beacon signals. Charts carry true and magnetic compass roses, latitude and longitude grid lines, location of all land masses, indication of prominent landmarks, depth of water, type of bottom, restricted areas, and locations of anchorage and dock areas, wrecks, sandbars, and reefs. They also denote the exact location and identifying characteristics of every aid-to-navigation marker. Obtain a copy of U. S. Coast & Geodetic Survey Chart No. 1 for a complete list of all symbols used on charts.

153 ᧤ What are "true" compass readings?

True compass readings are based on the "true" geographical North Pole. For example, a true compass reading of 90° is due east.

154 ᧤ What are "magnetic" compass readings?

Magnetic readings are based on the magnetic North Pole, which is not at the true North Pole.

155 ∾ What is compass variation?

The difference between true north and magnetic north is called "compass variation." In some areas, variation may change from year to year, but the direction and amount of shift is indicated on charts.

156 ∾ How are magnetic readings adjusted to true readings?

If variation is easterly, it is added to the magnetic reading to find the true reading. For example, if the variation is 3° east and the magnetic compass reading is 87°, the true reading is 90°. If the variation is westerly, it is subtracted from the magnetic reading to obtain the true reading. To adjust true readings to magnetic readings, subtract the easterly variation and add the westerly variation.

157 ∾ What is compass deviation?

Compass deviation is error produced by iron or steel aboard a boat that deflects the compass. Deviation varies with each boat.

158 ∽ How is compass deviation determined?

One way is to "swing ship" between two markers or
landmarks ashore where the correct magnetic bearing
is known. As the ship is turned around, the compass readings can be checked against the known bearing. Another
way is to make runs in each direction between markers
on a north-south line and then on an east-west line.

159 ∽ How is it possible to correct a compass for
      deviation?

Some compasses have built-in adjustment magnets. With
others, magnets are placed near the compass to cancel
out deviation as much as possible.

160 ∽ If a compass is corrected for deviation, but the
      correction is not complete, how can a further
      adjustment be made for this?

It is almost impossible to cancel out all deviation. Make
up a table of deviation that shows how far the compass
is off for at least 30° intervals. To correct to an accurate
magnetic reading, add the deviation or subtract from
the compass reading, as required.

161 ∽ What are "true" bearings?

True bearings are based on true geographic north. For example, if a boat is on a true heading of 50° and an object is sighted 35° to the right of the boat's bow, the true bearing of the object is 85°.

162 ❧ What are magnetic bearings?

Magnetic bearings are based on magnetic north. For example, if a boat is on a compass course of 50° (corrected for deviation) and an object is sighted 35° to the right of the boat's bow, the magnetic bearing of the object is 85°.

163 ❧ What are relative bearings?

Relative bearings are based on the fore-and-aft line of a boat, without regard to true or magnetic north. In 161 and 162, above, the relative bearing of the object sighted is 35°.

164 ❧ How is the position of a boat determined by taking bearings?

The simplest way is to take compass (magnetic) bearings on two or three objects, such as aids to navigation or prominent landmarks, that can be identified on the chart. (See Figure 6-4.) Using the magnetic compass rose on the chart as a guide, run your position lines through each of the objects. The intersection of the lines indicates your position.

165 ⚭ What is a pelorus?

A pelorus is a dummy compass fitted with a sight for taking bearings. Align the compass card with the ship's heading and align the sight on the object of the bearing. Read the bearing on the pelorus compass card.

166 ⚭ Can a sextant be used to take relative bearings?

Yes. Hold the instrument so that the handle is facing down. (See Figure 6–5.) Sight an object directly in front of the boat and pick up the object of bearing in the mirror. Move the sextant arm until the two objects are aligned and read the bearing on the sextant scale.

167 ⚭ How is a direction finder used to take bearings?

For this operation, you must use charts showing location, radio frequency, and code characteristics of marine beacons. Select and tune in a station. Adjust compass rose on the direction finder so that it matches the heading of boat. Turn antenna until no signal is heard (the null). Have the man at helm call out "mark" every time the boat is on its exact course. The reading on DF pointer when you have a null at the time "mark" is called gives the compass bearing of the station tuned.

168 ᴈᴎ If a powerboat and sailboat are on a converging course that could lead to collision, which boat has the right of way?

A boat under sail always has the right of way over a boat under power. If the powerboat is a towboat with barges, however, it is best for the sailboat to give way because the tow is not easy to maneuver. A boat under sail *and* power is governed by powerboat rules.

169 ᴈᴎ If two powerboats are approaching head on, what should they do?

Both boats must alter course to starboard and pass port to port.

170 ᴈᴎ If one powerboat is passing another on the same course, which boat has the right of way?

The boat that is being overtaken has the right of way; the overtaking vessel must keep clear.

171 ᴈᴎ If two boats are approaching each other at an angle of approximately 90°, which boat has the right of way?

The boat that is to the right of the other is the privileged vessel.

172 ⨍ If a sailboat on a beat to windward is approaching another sailboat running down wind on a collision course, which boat must give way?

The boat running free must give way. Because this ruling was originally based on the capabilities of square-rigged ships, many persons now feel that the reverse should become the correct practice. A boat running free may have to execute a dangerous jibe, but the boat on the wind can luff up, tack, or fall off to leeward quite easily.

173 ⨍ If two sailboats are approaching each other on different tacks, which boat has the right of way?

The boat on the starboard tack has the right of way.

174 ⨍ When two sailboats on the same tack are approaching each other on a collision course, which must keep clear?

The boat to windward is the burdened vessel and must keep clear.

175 ∞ What is the correct whistle signal to give to indicate that you intend to pass a boat ahead to port (i.e., leave it to your starboard)?

Two short blasts is the correct signal.

176 ∞ What is the whistle signal to give if you intend to pass to starboard (i.e., leave the boat you are overtaking to your port)?

Give one short blast of your whistle.

177 ∞ What is the correct way to answer a signal?

If the maneuver can be executed without danger, answer with the same signal as the one given.

178 ∞ What whistle signal should be given as an answer if the original signal is not understood or if the maneuver would be dangerous to execute?

Four or more short blasts is the danger signal, and it is given in these cases.

179 ∞ What is the correct fog signal for a powerboat under way?

Give one long blast of the horn or whistle every 60 seconds.

180 ∞ What is the correct fog signal for a power-boat with a tow, such as a tugboat with barges?

A long blast followed by two short blasts indicates a boat with tow.

181 ∞ What is the correct fog signal for a sailboat on the starboard tack?

Give one short blast every 60 seconds.

182 ∞ What is the fog signal for a sailboat on the port tack?

Give two short blasts every 60 seconds.

183 ∞ What fog signal should a sailboat give when running free?

Three short blasts every 60 seconds is the correct fog signal when running free.

184 ∽ What fog signal should be given by an anchored boat?

Ring a bell rapidly every 60 seconds.

185 ∽ What is a diaphone signal?

A diaphone signal is given in fog by such aids to navigation as lighthouses and lightships. If the signal has two tones, the second tone is always lower than the first.

186 ∽ What other sound signals are given in fog by aids to navigation?

Other "reduced-visibility audio aids" include diaphragm horns (including duplex or triplex horns that produce a "chime" signal), reed horns, sirens, whistles, and bells. All are identified on U. S. Coast & Geodetic Survey charts.

187 ∽ What navigation lights are required for power-boats under 26 feet in length under international rules?

The requirements are a 20-point combination red (port) and green (starboard) light at the bow, visible for at least 1 mile; a 20-point white light located at least 3 feet higher than the combination light, visible for 3 miles, and a 12-point white light at the stern, visible for at least 2 miles.

188 ∽ What navigation lights are required for power-boats under 26 feet in length operating under inland rules?

The requirements here are a 20-point red-and-green combination light at the bow, visible at least 1 mile away and an all-around white light at the stern, mounted higher than the combination light at the bow, which must be visible for a minimum of 2 miles.

189 ∽ What are the required navigation lights under international rules for a boat more than 26 feet long?

Boats of more than 26 feet in length and under 40 gross tons displacement must carry a 10-point red (port) light, a 10-point green (starboard) light, a 20-point white light forward, at least 3 feet higher than the red and green lights, and a 12-point stern light. Both red and green lights must be visible for 1 mile; the 20-point white light must be visible for 3 miles; and the 12-point stern light must be visible for 2 miles.

190 ∾ Under inland rules, what are the required navigation lights for a powerboat of more than 26 feet in length?

Four lights must be carried: a 20-point white light near the stem, visible for 2 miles; a 10-point red (port) light visible for 1 mile; a 10-point green light (starboard) visible for 1 mile; and an all-around white light at the stern, higher than the 20-point forward light and visible for 2 miles.

191 ∾ What are the required navigation lights under international rules for sailboats under 26 feet in length?

A 20-point combination red-and-green light at the bow is required, visible for 1 mile, along with a 12-point white light at the stern, visible for 2 miles.

192 ∾ What are the required navigation lights for a sailboat under 26 feet in length operating under inland rules?

There must be carried a 20-point combination red-and-green light at the bow, visible for 1 mile, plus an all-around white light to be shown at the stern when being overtaken.

193 ໖ Under international rules, what navigation lights are required for a sailboat more than 26 feet in length?

A 10-point red (port) light visible for 1 mile, a 10-point green (starboard) light visible for 1 mile, and a 12-point stern light visible for 2 miles are required.

194 ໖ What are the required navigation lights for a sailboat more than 26 feet in length operating under inland rules?

The three requirements are a 10-point red (port) light visible for 1 mile, a 10-point starboard (green) light visible for 1 mile, and an all-around white light to be shown at the stern when being overtaken.

195 ໖ If a boat operates on both inland and international waters, which light system should be used?

Use the lights required under international rules.

CHAPTER

～7～

CRUISING
TECHNIQUES

EXPERTS

Ann Davison
Jim Emmett
Ellison Michel
Elbert Robberson
Nicholas Rosa
John Whiting

Once a boatman becomes familiar with the waters near his home, he looks for new places. With the proper cooking and sleeping equipment aboard, even modest runabouts can be used for extended camping and cruising. Here are the answers to the questions most frequently asked on this subject.

196 ∾ What gear and supplies are considered essential
for a weekend cruise?

Cruise supplies depend on the size of the boat, the type
of cruise planned, and the number of persons who will
take part. The boat should be fitted with all required
equipment and lights. Take along a first-aid kit and
manual, engine tools and spare parts, and other emergency gear such as signaling devices. Stow aboard food,
ice, beverages, bedding, and clothing to meet all possible
weather conditions.

197 ∾ Have you any suggestions for stowing the many
small items that tend to clutter up a boat?

Ann Davison, who sailed across the Atlantic Ocean alone
in a small sloop, has worked out a couple of rigs that are
handy. One is to make up small canvas bags that can be
hung in the cabin. Another rig is to use shock-cord lash-
ings for items that should be kept handy, such as flash-
lights. Pullman hammocks suspended in a cabin can
carry a great deal of gear.

198 ∾ What is the proper way to stow food in a boat?

Use a crayon or grease pencil to mark the contents of
canned goods on the lids of the cans; if the labels get wet

and soak off, you will still know what is in the cans. Stow canned goods in lockers under bunks. Bottled beverages can be stowed under the floor boards. Baked goods should be kept high and dry. Keep perishables on ice.

199 ๛ How should meals for a cruise be planned?

Plan in advance the menu for every meal to be served. If a cruise is for several days or more, plan to take just enough perishables to last from one stop for ice until the next. Precook as many foods as possible at home to reduce time in the galley. When planning menus, remember that shoreside appetites show surprising increases on the water.

200 ๛ What special safety precautions should be taken to protect small children aboard boats?

Life jackets in good condition and of the proper size should be worn by youngsters when on deck at all times when the boat is under way. (See Figure 7–1.) The smallest tots can be put into a "harness" available at childrens' stores and tied to a line that will enable them to move about the cockpit. Do not let children "horse around" on boats. Keep them off the foredeck and do not let them climb or stand where they might fall overboard. Keep an eye on children around docks, too.

201 ∽ Have you any suggestions for safety precautions that can be taken before leaving on a cruise?

Thoroughly check all required safety equipment: life preservers, fire extinguishers, signal devices for day and night, radio equipment, and first-aid kit. It's also a good idea to give the Coast Guard your planned course, destination, and estimated time of arrival. Then, if you do not arrive at your destination within a reasonable time, the Coast Guard will institute a search.

202 ∽ How should crew work be organized on a cruise?

On a family trip, work should be divided according to the capacity of the members to perform assigned duties. Children, especially, should be drilled in their chores. If a group of adults are cruising, divide your crew into "watches" to share in all chores, including handling the boat, cooking, and cleaning.

203 ∽ What is the best way to protect against sunburn?

Avoid overexposure; wear a hat that will protect your nose and ears. Unless you have a good sun tan, wear clothing that will protect your arms and legs. Use a good sun-tan lotion, which will give some measure of protection against the sun's rays.

204 ⌒ What is the best way to protect eyes against sun glare?

Particularly in the morning and evening, glare can make piloting difficult and uncomfortable. Wear dark sunglasses of good, optical-quality glass, or Polaroid sunglasses. Tinted contact lenses can also be used.

205 ⌒ What sort of clothes should be worn on a cruise?

This depends on the time, the boat, and the place. For cruising on a large yacht in the Mediterranean, for example, the most expensive sportswear available would be just the thing. In general, wear comfortable clothes that can take an occasional wetting and take enough to allow for changes. You might want to take along swimsuits and casual or dress shore clothes. Take along foul-weather gear, including heavy sweaters or jackets if you think the weather might turn cold.

206 ⌒ How far should one go on a day's cruising?

If facilities for fuel, ice, food, and mooring are plentiful along your route, your run can be from early morning until fairly late in the evening. Otherwise, plan each day's run so that you will not still be searching at 1 A.M. for a good location to tie up for the night or take on supplies.

207 ᐁ How should a mooring be selected at a strange marina?

In most instances the dock attendant will assign a berth. Otherwise, choose an area that is as protected as possible from weather and waterway traffic.

208 ᐁ What is the best way to select an anchorage?

Check the weather forecast and examine your chart. Choose an anchorage that will offer a firm holding for your hook and good protection from anticipated weather conditions. Remember to allow for tide and current conditions. Do not anchor in channels or fairways.

209 ᐁ What is the proper procedure if the weather turns bad while one is cruising?

In a bad blow, head for the nearest shelter. Always check your weather reports before starting out; it may be better to remain at an anchorage or dock for a day or two than to take a pounding on open water.

210 ∾ What weather instruments do you recommend
for a boat on a cruise?

It is a good idea to include the following items in your
cruise gear: a portable radio, a barometer, a thermometer,
a sling psychrometer, weather maps from the newspaper,
a Guest Weathercaster, and a cloud chart or chapter on
clouds from a weather book.

211 ∾ How is a barometer used?

A barometer records atmospheric pressure, which
changes as frontal systems approach an area. The words
rain, change, and *fair* that are usually found on barometers should be ignored—the change in the reading is the
important thing. A rise or fall in pressure indicates a
change in the weather from existing conditions. If pressure falls rapidly, it indicates the approach of a storm.
If pressure falls rapidly and far, it indicates a storm of
hurricane intensity. Unfortunately, in this latter case
particularly, by the time the pressure is at its lowest point
you are in the middle of the storm.

212 ∾ What is a sling psychrometer, and how is it
used?

A sling psychrometer is made up of two mercury ther-
mometers mounted on a common backing and hung from
a pivoted handle. One thermometer has a clean muslin

"sock" that covers the bulb. When a reading is taken, the sock is wetted with fresh water and the instrument is twirled by the handle for 15 or 20 seconds. This thermometer then records a lower temperature than the other, dry-bulb thermometer. Looking up the difference between the readings on a table supplied with the instrument enables one to find the "dew point" for the dry-bulb-recorded temperature.

If the air temperature is falling, as indicated by regular checks, and if the dew point remains the same, there is a possibility of fog. For example, if air temperature is 85°, and the dew point is 70°, and the temperature is falling at the rate of 2 degrees an hour, fog will form in 2½ hours if the temperature continues to drop.

213 ∾ How is the thermometer used in weather observations?

In simple use of the thermometer on a boat, watch for sudden drops in temperature. This could indicate approaching bad weather. This rule by itself will not give a good forecast, but it often fits in with other observations.

214 ∾ How is the Guest Weathercaster used?

This is a little book that has a four-way dial on the front cover. The dials are set for sky condition, barometer change, barometer reading, and wind direction. A reading is obtained which is checked against tables in the book to provide an accurate forecast. The book is available through yacht-supply stores.

215 ∾ How is a cloud chart used as a weather aid?

This helps the boatman to learn the names of the various types of clouds and to understand what is happening when weather conditions change—thus, changes in local weather can be predicted.

216 ∾ How are weather maps from newspapers used as a forecasting aid?

By following the shape and movement of frontal areas for a few days prior to the start of a cruise, it is possible to anticipate the type of weather to be expected on the cruise.

217 ∾ What equipment is required for cruising at night?

Carry navigation lights as required by law, a good searchlight, a flashlight, a compass, and charts for your area. A lead line for taking soundings is a good thing to take along, as are emergency signal flares.

218 ∞ What are the recommended procedures for night cruising?

Before darkness sets in, plan the courses you will be following. Pick courses that are as free of obstacles as possible and keep track of your running time. Shield the helmsman from bright lights that could interfere with his vision. Keep a searchlight and binoculars handy. Review the required lights for other pleasure craft, tows, barges, and other commercial boats. Check a current light list to aid in identifying channel-marker lights.

219 ∞ What equipment should be carried on a boat for cruising by day and camping out at night?

A tent, air mattresses, sleeping bags, a sharp hatchet, a handful of nails, a water container, a small cooking grill (see Figure 7–2), canned heat, and litter bags are recommended for camping when cruising.

220 ∞ Where on a boat should the various flags and pennants be flown?

The yacht ensign is flown at the stern of a powerboat or a sailboat under power. A sloop or a schooner under sail can fly the ensign from the leech of the mainsail; on a ketch or yawl, the ensign can be flown from the leech of the mizzensail. The owner's private signal is flown from the starboard spreaders, and the club pennant is flown from the masthead.

221 ⚭ How does one "dress ship"?

Alphabet and numeral pennants are run from the stem to the masthead and back down to the transom. There is no special sequence for the flags—they are usually mixed by color and shape.

MONEY-SAVING TIPS

EXPERTS

**Boating and Accessory
    Manufacturers**
Boating Associations
The U. S. Coast Guard

Here are free, informative sources on a wide range of boating subjects, from boat selection to cruising tips, maintenance, and rules of the road. These are the booklets that will help you get more enjoyment from your boating and, in many cases, offer money-saving hints for boat and equipment improvements.

222 ∾ What is a source of comprehensive information on selecting a boat for a family?

Write for the booklet "Family Boating Is Fun," available from the National Association of Engine and Boat Manufacturers, Inc., 420 Lexington Avenue, New York 17, New York.

223 ∾ Where is there available full information on choosing an anchor?

Write to Danforth Anchors, 216 Allston Way, Berkeley 4, California, for the booklet, "Anchors and Anchoring."

224 ∾ Is there any organization that will give advice on the care of diesel engines?

Write for "Fuel Oil and High RPM Diesel Engines," available from Detroit Diesel Engine Division, General Motors Corporation, 13400 West Outer Drive, Detroit 28, Michigan.

225 ∾ Where can complete information be obtained on choosing a propeller for an outboard rig?

Write to Columbian Bronze Corporation, Freeport, New York, and to the Michigan Wheel Company, Grand Rapids, Michigan, for selector charts and catalogs.

226 ∞ Are there any aids available for the selection of a radiotelephone?

Write for the booklet "Modern Marine Radiotelephones and How To Choose Them," available from Pearce-Simpson, Inc., 2295 Northwest 14th Street, Miami 35, Florida.

227 ∞ Water skis are made in different shapes and sizes for general skiing, for slalom skiing, and for jumping. What type of skis are best for each purpose?

A water-ski selection chart from White Bear Water Ski Company gives complete information. The company is located at 5315 Bald Eagle Boulevard, West, White Bear Lake 10, Minnesota.

228 ∞ Are there any booklets on choosing the right type of lines for rigging a sailboat?

"How To Use Rope," from Plymouth Cordage Company, Plymouth, Massachusetts, and "Nylon and Dacron in Yachting Lines," from E. I. du Pont de Nemours & Company, 5518 Nemours Building, Wilmington 98, Delaware, are booklets that give complete information on choice of lines.

229 ⌘ Where is there available maintenance advice for steel-hull cruiser construction?

Write to E. W. & A. P. Dupont Company, Patterson, Louisiana, for their informative "Safti-Craft Maintenance Manual."

230 ⌘ Is there any source of information on cleaning the gas tank on a boat?

Write for the booklet "You Can Remove Gum Deposits from Your Gas Tank," available from Gulf Oil Corporation, 17 Battery Place, New York 4, New York.

231 ⌘ Before overhauling the carburetor on an inboard gasoline engine it is desirable to secure information on carburetor operation. Is this available?

A good guide on the subject is the booklet "Know Your Carburetor," which can be secured by writing to Pennsylvania Refining Company, 2686 Lisbon Road, Cleveland 4, Ohio.

232 ⌘ What is a source of information on plywood boat construction?

The pamphlet "How To Select and Build with Plywood" is published by the Douglas Fir Plywood Association, Tacoma 2, Washington.

233 ∞ Is there a booklet that gives information on the treatment of wood to prevent dry rot?

Write to Darworth, Inc., Chemical Products Division, Simsbury, Connecticut, for their booklet on "Wood Preservatives."

234 ∞ In removing the old finish from a boat and repainting the whole works, what type of paint should be used for each job—topsides, deck, bottom, and interior?

"Boat Painting Helps," published by the International Paint Company, 21 West Street, New York 6, New York, gives comprehensive painting information.

235 ∞ Is there an organization which can supply information on the properties of anti-fouling bottom paint?

Write to Metallic Coatings Corporation, 919 North Michigan Avenue, Chicago 11, Illinois, for the pamphlet "Anti-Fouling Bottom Coatings."

236 ⟳ Is there a source of information on making repairs to a fiberglass boat hull?

Two booklets are available: "How To Use a Fiberglass Repair Kit," from Glass Plastics Corporation, 1605 West Elizabeth Avenue, Linden, New Jersey; and "How to Repair Your Boat with a Cordoglas Speedkit," from Cordo Chemical Corporation, 34 Smith Street, Norwalk, Connecticut.

237 ⟳ Where is there available information on covering a boat with fiberglass?

Booklets on this subject can be obtained from Neehi Protective Coatings, Inc., 340 West Hoffman Avenue, Lindenhurst, New York; International Paint Company, 21 West Street, New York 6, New York, and Owens Corning Fiberglas Corporation, 717 Fifth Avenue, New York 22, New York.

238 ⟳ Are there any suggestions on how to get the most enjoyment from ownership of an outboard runabout?

Write for the booklet "More Fun on the Water," available from the National Association of Engine and Boat Manufacturers, 420 Lexington Avenue, New York 17, New York.

239 ∾ Where is there available information on fishing
from an outboard craft?

Write for "Outboard Fishing," which can be secured
from Evinrude Motors, 4119 North 27th Street, Milwaukee 16, Wisconsin.

240 ∾ What is a source of general information on how
to use an outboard and trailer rig?

"Outboard Handling," available from the Outboard
Boating Club of America, 307 North Michigan Avenue,
Chicago 1, Illinois, is a handy guide for the use of boats,
motors, and trailers.

241 ∾ What is a source of information on how to
water ski?

Write for the booklet "Water Skiing," available from
Evinrude Motors, 4119 North 27th Street, Milwaukee
16, Wisconsin.

242 ∾ Our nearest lake is about 35 miles away, but
we want to buy a boat, motor, and trailer rig.
Where can we obtain information on how to
use a trailer?

"How To Load and Carry Small Boats" is a helpful booklet available from Arkansas Traveler, 2065 East 14th Street, Little Rock, Arkansas.

243 ✀ Where can a local group secure information on setting up by-laws, activities program, and so on, for a boat club?

Write for "How To Organize for More Fun Afloat," available from the Outboard Boating Club of America, 307 North Michigan Avenue, Chicago 1, Illinois.

244 ✀ Some states grant a tax refund on marine gas purchases. How can this refund be applied for?

Write for the "Gas Tax Refund Bulletin," available from Socony-Mobil Oil Company, 150 East 42nd Street, New York 17, New York.

245 ✀ Who has available information about the types of insurance available for pleasure craft and the coverage extended by the various policies?

The booklet "The ABC of Yacht Insurance," published by Chubb & Son, 90 John Street, New York 38, New York, has this information.

246 ∽ What are the sources of information on protecting the metal fastenings on a boat against corrosion?

Write for the booklet "What Every Boat Owner Should Know," available from The International Nickel Co., 67 Wall Street, New York 5, New York.

247 ∽ Does the Coast Guard publish information on its requirements for numbering boats?

Write the U. S. Coast Guard, Washington 25, D.C., for "Rules and Regulations for Numbering Boats."

248 ∽ Where can there be secured a complete rundown of legal equipment requirements for small boats?

Write for the pamphlet "Legal Requirements for Boats," published by the U. S. Coast Guard, Washington 25, D.C.

249 ∽ Is there a complete listing of rules of the road for boats?

Write to the U. S. Coast Guard, Washington 25, D.C., for "Rules of the Road."

250 ∽ I have a large cruiser that I would like to use for carrying sightseers. What legal requirements must be met for the operation of a large cruiser for carrying sightseers?

Write for the pamphlet "Rules and Regulations for Boats Carrying Passengers," available from the U. S. Coast Guard, Washington 25, D.C.

BOAT AND ACCESSORIES BUYER'S GUIDE

On the following pages are check lists that can be used when selecting a new or used boat, marine engines, deck hardware and fittings, and navigation aids and equipment.

These lists, reprinted here with permission from the 1960 Buying Guide and Marine Directory issue of Popular Boating *Magazine*, are designed to provide a handy reference that should simplify selection of the proper boat and equipment for your needs. Proper use of these check lists will eliminate the headaches and heartaches that can occur when a wrong choice is made.

OUTBOARD BOATS

Outboard-powered craft are by far the most popular type of boat operating in this country today, and with good reason. Low initial cost, ease of operation, and portability make them the favorites with people on a relatively low budget, those who are new to the sport, and those who must trail their boats to the nearest waterways. Also, there is such a wide selection of types, sizes, and construction that it is possible to select an outboard boat that meets the needs of every boating family.

☐ Is the boat you are considering made by a recognized boat builder?

☐ Have you discussed performance with owners of similar models?

☐ Is this a style which has proven seaworthy and popular on your local waterways?

☐ Has the construction material (wood, canvas, metal, fiberglass) proved to be durable and in need of minimum maintenance in your area?

☐ Will it trailer easily?

HULL SPEED

☐ Does this boat have a reputation for top performance using recommended horsepower?

☐ Is it specifically recommended for water skiing?

☐ Can the transom take twin motors, if desired?

☐ Is the boat recommended for planing speeds, or is it a heavier displacement type?

☐ Is it known to handle well in turns, or does the chine tend to trip it?

HULL SAFETY

☐ Is there enough freeboard and stability so that waves will not wash aboard?

☐ Is the transom cut out 20 inches for the safer long-shaft motors?

☐ Is there a self-bailing motor well?

☐ Is the windshield of safety glass or shatterproof plastic?

☐ Is adequate flotation provided, preferably under the decks, so that the boat will not capsize if swamped?

☐ Is the transom firmly installed with knees, breast hooks, and braces so that it can handle the thrust of the motors?

ACCOMMODATIONS

☐ Can passengers sleep aboard?

☐ Can a top be rigged for sun, rain, and mosquito protection?

☐ If the boat is an outboard cruiser, does it have a marine toilet?

☐ Does it come with legally required lights, life preservers, fire extinguishers, and other safety equipment?

☐ Is there storage area for extra gas cans, battery, anchor, and lines?

INBOARD BOATS

Inboard-engine-powered boats offer the powerboat enthusiast a wide range of sizes, types, and styles, from open skiffs to the ultimate in large luxury cruisers containing practically all the household conveniences available.

☐ Is this boat suitable for your local waters? Is it suitable for longer trips you may want to take?

☐ Is she similar to craft you have already handled so that you (and your family) will feel comfortable about your ability to skipper her?

☐ Does the builder have a well-established reputation?

☐ Can the dealer refer you to other satisfied owners?

HULL

☐ Have hulls of this type proved stable and "seakindly" in your local waters?

☐ Have the materials (wood, metal, or plastic) stood up well in your area?

☐ Is it easy to repair?

☐ Do boats of this type have good resale value?

☐ For the number of years you expect to keep the boat, does the design have styling which will continue to be pleasing, or will it become outmoded rapidly?

ENGINES

☐ Will your choice of power give you the speed and cruising range you will require?

☐ Can your purchase be budgeted to allow for twin-engine installation for added safety and maneuverability?

☐ Does the motor manufacturer have an established reputation and good repair and servicing facilities in your area?

ACCOMMODATIONS

☐ Are both cockpit and cabin accommodations adequate for family entertaining and cruising?

☐ Can the cabin be kept warm in cold weather and well ventilated and screened when it's hot?

☐ Is your choice "fully found," or will a great many items of equipment and accessories be required?

SAILBOATS

The thrill of sailing is a sensation that is hard to beat. The feeling of satisfaction after bringing your boat to anchor in a strange harbor, utilizing only the power of the wind and your own skill, ability, and knowledge of tides and currents is one of the greatest joys of boating.

☐ Is this boat suitable for your local waters?

☐ Is she suitable for longer trips you may want to take?

☐ Is she similar to craft you have already sailed so that you (and your family) will feel comfortable about your ability to handle her?

☐ Does the builder have a well-established reputation?

☐ Can the dealer refer you to other satisfied owners?

☐ Can the boat be sailed singlehanded?

HULL

☐ Have hulls of this type proved stable and "seakindly" in your local waters?

☐ Have the materials (wood, metal, or plastic) stood up well in your area?

☐ Will the boat be fairly easy to repair and maintain?

☐ Do boats of this type have good resale value?

RIGGING AND SAILS

☐ Have rigging materials (stainless steel, Monel, or plow steel) stood up well in your area?

☐ Has allowance been made for rigging adjustments?

☐ Can her sails be handled easily by your family or regular crew?

☐ Are her sails (cotton, Dacron, or Nylon) made by an established sailmaker?

☐ Are sails included in the price of the boat?

RACING BOATS

☐ Are there enough boats of the same class in your area so that there will be interesting and continued competition?

☐ Do the hull, sails, and rigging of your craft meet specifications for the class?

☐ Is she equipped with light racing blocks?

☐ Does she have enough sails to meet all racing requirements?

CRUISING BOATS

☐ Are cockpit and cabin accommodations adequate for family entertaining and cruising?

☐ Can the cabin be kept at a comfortable temperature in cold weather and well-ventilated and screened when it turns warm?

☐ Is the boat "fully found," or will she require the addition of a great many items of accessories and equipment?

☐ Does she have an auxiliary engine (gasoline or diesel)?

☐ Are good service and repair facilities for the engine available in your area?

☐ In a blow, will she be safe and reasonably comfortable for you and your family?

SPECIALTY CRAFT

Dinghies, skiffs, canoes, houseboats, novelty boats, and racing craft are all designed for special purposes. Whether you want a pedal-powered water scooter or a floating home, the boat should be well-built, safe for the waters on which it is to be used, and easy to handle.

☐ Is this boat suitable for your local waters?
☐ Is it a "stunt" boat that may be enjoyable once or twice, but one which you may tire of quickly?
☐ Is it similar to craft you have already sailed so that you will feel sure about your ability to handle it?
☐ Does the builder have a well-established reputation?
☐ Can the dealer refer you to other satisfied owners?

HULL

☐ Have hulls of this type proved stable and "seakindly" in your local waters?
☐ Have the materials (wood, metal, or plastic) stood up well in your area?
☐ Is it easy to repair and maintain?
☐ Do boats of its type have good resale value?

POWER

☐ Has provision been made for equipping the craft with outboard or inboard power, if so desired?
☐ Is there room to store adequate gas for a trip?
☐ Will full power make her difficult for youngsters to handle?

ACCOMMODATIONS

☐ Can passengers use the craft for its special purpose and still be comfortable aboard?

☐ Is there provision for shelter during inclement weather?

☐ Is there room for all required and recommended safety equipment aboard, and can it be stowed so it will not be lost overboard?

☐ Is your choice "fully found," or will a great many additional items of equipment be required?

MARINE ENGINES

Unless yours is a sailboat, you are completely dependent upon the power plant. Marine engines, both inboard and outboard, have been refined, improved, and re-engineered in the past 5 years or so—enough so that faultless operation is taken for granted by the boatman. Recent ocean crossings, and long-distance races have further proven engine dependability for prolonged running.

☐ Do you have enough experience to match an inboard or outboard motor to a boat? If not, can you secure the services of a reliable dealer?

☐ What kind of service will you expect from a power plant—economy of operation, or high-speed performance?

☐ Will an inboard engine or outboard motor best fit your requirements?

☐ Remember that engine weight affects the trim of a boat. Is your engine weight tailored to the hull?

☐ Will you be able to do your own maintenance? (If not, a detachable motor simplifies repairs.)

☐ Will you trail your boat, or it is moored afloat?

OUTBOARDS

☐ High-horsepower motors are frequently unsuited for small boats. Can your dealer advise you?

☐ Do you wish to enter the racing field, or cruise at slower speeds?

☐ Will the children operate the motor?

☐ Is the engine electric-starting or manual?

☐ Would twin engines better fill your needs?

INBOARDS

☐ Have your measured the available space for a new installation?

☐ Would a Vee-drive help to conserve valuable space? Would reduction gears improve performance?

☐ What cruising range would you like to attain?

☐ What kind of service will the engine be required to perform?

☐ Have you checked with your dealer to see if he will accept a trade-in on your old engine?

HARDWARE AND FITTINGS

Marine hardware is designed for the rugged use the sea demands from fittings. To purchase house hardware and expect it to perform well under conditions of salt spray and the accelerated corrosion of marine use is to invite trouble. In sailboat service, especially, the substitution of inferior fittings and fastenings to save money is ill-advised. The stresses, loads, and thrust in a sailboat's rigging demand the best possible quality obtainable and a built-in safety factor beyond the requirements of normal use. These safety factors do not necessarily imply greater weight. New Nylon and composition fittings combine strength with light weight, and titanium and aluminum alloys are available in a wide range of fittings carefully designed for specialized uses.

☐ Are you using the right hardware and fittings for the right job?

☐ Are cleats and fairleads heavy enough, and are they securely through-bolted to hold your boat in a severe blow?

☐ Have you checked the fabric of your life preservers for rips and dry rot?

☐ Are your cabin fittings securely fastened so that they cannot break loose in heavy seas?

ANCHORS AND MOORINGS

☐ Is your ground tackle suited to the bottom where you operate?

☐ Is your anchor heavy enough for all the conditions of wind and weather you are likely to encounter? Do you carry a spare?

☐ Do your carry spare anchor keys and shackles?

☐ Have you marked off your anchor lines so that you know how much scope is out?

HANDY EQUIPMENT

☐ Do you have a permanently mounted bilge pump, and do you frequently check its operation?

☐ Do you have an adequate supply of docking fenders to save your topside paint job?

☐ "Fully found" is an old phrase that describes a boat well equipped for comfort and safety and not lacking in any essential equipment. Does your boat qualify?

NAVIGATION AIDS AND EQUIPMENT

When the dock lines are made up and you are under way, the task of navigating your boat begins. No matter how short the run, even if you can see the shore, a knowledge of navigation is necessary. In fact, the closer to shore you are, the more important the art of piloting becomes. Fog can close in at any time, and currents can upset calculations. The boatman who doesn't bother to learn the rudiments of navigation is denying himself one of the most pleasant aspects of boating.

☐ Are you fully aware of the complete range of navigating aids available to boatmen?

☐ Do you consider accurate piloting "just a tedious chore," or do you exploit navigation as one of the pleasures of boating?

☐ Have you taken advantage of the cost-free organizations that teach piloting and navigation, such as the U. S. Power Squadrons and the Coast Guard Auxiliary?

☐ Have you taught your wife, or habitual cruising partner, enough rudimentary navigation to bring the boat safely home in case you are incapacitated?

COMPASSES AND CHARTS

☐ A Government chart is an aid to navigation. Has reading one become second instinct to you?

☐ Is the buoyage system of the United States familiar to you?

☐ Do you "boat by the seat of your pants," or are you able and willing to utilize a reliable compass?

☐ Does a pea-soup fog scare you, or does it present an opportunity to practice with confidence the principles you have learned?

RADIO AIDS

☐ Is the nature of your cruising such that a good RDF will prove a valuable adjunct to your equipment?

☐ Do you understand the principle and operation of a Depthometer?

☐ Can you correct an RDF bearing for plotting on a mercator chart?

☐ Radar, Loran, RDF, Depthfinders and gyro-compasses are all now available for the small boat. Do you need any of these?

NAVIGATING ACCESSORIES

☐ Do you have a pair of good binoculars to use as a navigating aid?

☐ If you struggle with mathematics, could you use an inexpensive and simple time-speed-distance calculator?

☐ A course protractor or parallel rulers, dividers, pencil, eraser, and compass constitute the minimum equipment necessary aboard any boat. Do you have all of them?